Life in Transit

Favourite Travel & Tribute Poems

By Wayne Visser

Second Edition

I0098776

Second paperback edition published in 2016 by Kaleidoscope Futures, London, UK.

First paperback edition published in 2014 by Wayne Visser. First and second electronic edition published in 2014 by Wayne Visser and in 2016 by Kaleidoscope Futures.

Printing and distribution by Lulu.com.

ISBN 978-1-908875-30-3

Dedication

In memory of my spiritual mentor, Bob
Steyn, and my dear friend, Karen Weinberg

Fiction Books by Wayne Visser

Non-fiction Books by Wayne Visser

Beyond Reasonable Greed

South Africa: Reasons to Believe

Corporate Citizenship in Africa

Business Frontiers

The A to Z of Corporate Social
Responsibility

Making A Difference

Landmarks for Sustainability

The Top 50 Sustainability Books

The World Guide to CSR

The Age of Responsibility

The Quest for Sustainable Business

Corporate Sustainability & Responsibility

CSR 2.0

Disrupting the Future

This is Tomorrow

Sustainable Frontiers

The CSR International Research
Compendium

The World Guide to Sustainable Enterprise

About the Author

Wayne Visser was born in Zimbabwe and has lived most of his life in South Africa and the UK. He is a writer, academic, social entrepreneur, professional speaker and amateur artist.

Wayne sees travel – the places visited and the people encountered – as the real university of life. His views on travel are best summed up in his own words:

Ultimately, travel delivers its promise
Taking us to new, undiscovered worlds
But never the ones we expected

Website: www.waynevisser.com
Email: wayne@waynevisser.com

Contents

Life in Transit

Life is lived in the in-between
In transit
Between coming and going
Between staying and moving on
Between here and there

And what we call home
What we call settled or contented
Is merely a resting place
A station for refuelling
A nexus for re-connecting
A junction for changing direction

The bus stops and train stations
The airports and traffic lights of our life
Are nodes linking us to our past
And windows peering into our future
They are choice matrixes
And platforms of destiny

At life's stopping points
We bump into others and smile
(Or curse silently under our breath)
We pause long enough to reflect
To mull on our confusion
And share moments of clarity

So let us not be so impatient to leave
To wish we were somewhere else
Because life's most unexpected surprises
Happen in the in-between
In the moments of passing touch
And the tangled knots of transition
Between boredom and panic
In the zone of chance
When the landscape is not rushing by

And love (the greatest surprise of all)
Is only to be found where paths cross
And journeys are re-routed
Where our most fixed plans change
And new destinations are contemplated

Love is seldom found at high speed

When we are looking for obvious landmarks

But rather when we are standing still
     enough

To notice subtle shifts in moods and
     patterns

Life is lived in the in-between

Amidst strangers who become friends

And friends who become lovers

Amidst lovers who become soul mates

And soul mates who make life worth living

And the places we think of as our endpoints

Are just launch pads for new beginnings

The time we spend waiting for our lives to
     change

Is the very fulcrum on which our galaxies
     pivot

Therefore, let us pay attention to the
     waiting

And be alert in the places of transit

Let us soak up the chaotic ambience of
    where we are

Rather than pine for the neatly ordered
    vision

Of where we could or should or want to be

Let us be where we are

Noticing the people and the smells

And the noise of the jumbled waiting

Alert to the feelings and the flow

And the beauty of the to-ing and fro-ing

Content not to be where we think we are
    going

Nor where we imagine we came from

Let us be happily in the transit of now

Fascinated by the overlapping of our world
    with others'

Of precious moments shared

Of fleeting smiles and knowing looks

Of orbits crossing that almost certainly
    mean nothing

And yet might just mean everything

Let us acknowledge all the forgettable faces

That emerge from the fog and melt back
     into oblivion

The warmth offered by random strangers

That leave us certain of nothing

Except that nothing is certain

And knowing no one

(Not even ourselves)

And yet knowing many so intimately

Through these fleeting connections

Life is lived in the in-between

Between moving and minding

Between loving and doubting

Between you and me

In transit

Life is lived

In the in-between

Generation Found

Once I was a boy soldier –
Now I'm shooting hoops
I'm not the generation lost
I'm bright and landing scoops

Once I was a girl servant –
Now I'm skipping ropes
I'm not the generation lost
I'm proud and full of hopes

Once I was a phantom child –
Now I'm quite a star
I'm not the generation lost
I'm strong and will go far

Once I was a nut to crack –
Now I'm acorn's tree
I'm not the generation lost
I'm growing tall and free

Once I was a ghetto kid –
Now I'm a go-getter
I'm not the generation lost
I'm good and getting better

We Rise, We Shine

Tribute to Maya Angelou (1928-2014)

When giants fall –
True heroes like Mandela
And timeless muses like Angelou –
The whole earth gasps
And shudders as one;
Convulsions reverberate
Deep in our hearts
Wide in our minds
And high in our souls –
As well they should
For no quake is greater
Than when spiritual giants fall

When I fall (or you) –
Whether from a stumble, a leap
Or a gentle ebbing away –
The world will be spared
Any collective tremors or sighs;

A precious few will notice
And smile through their tears
Yet my ordinary life (or yours)
Will be no less extraordinary
For all our numbered days
Leave remarkable impressions
On the soft clay of history

Meanwhile, we rise –
Inspired to tread the causeway
Of giants, be they standing or fallen –
We rise to embrace life
And conjure our dreams
We rise to see further
And take the next vital step
We rise to lift others
And weave the web of hope
We rise to show what's possible
Yes! Like our resilient Maya
Still, we rise. Surely, we shine

Thirty Four

Thirty four today
And I'm beginning to understand
How life creeps up on you
How, before you know it
Looking from the outside
You are no longer a child
Yet, knowing on the inside
You have barely been born

Thirty four today
And I'm beginning to understand
How life happens to you
How, in every moment
Gathered around the fireside
You are telling your story
Yet, even as the narrator
You don't know the next word

Thirty four today
And I'm beginning to understand

How life is full of surprises
How, when you least expect it
In the blink of an eye
You find the scenery changed
Yet, beneath the surface
You draw from a constant stream

Thirty four today
And I'm beginning to understand
How life can hurt sometimes
How, despite the armour
When the arrows pierce
You bleed like everyone else
Yet, one breath at a time
You have the strength to carry on

Thirty four today
And I'm beginning to understand
How life is art made real
How, even as an amateur
Splashing light and colour
You can create a masterpiece

Yet, when you look up
You see that beauty is reflected

Thirty four today
And I'm beginning to understand
How life is only the stage
How, no matter what the props
In the unfolding drama
You are there to learn loving
Yet, when the curtain falls
You find love outlasts all encores

Thirty four today
And I'm beginning to understand
How life is a fragile thing
How, like a child on the beach
When the tide changes
You must let the castles wash away
Yet, if you crafted with care
You dwell forever in the heart of life

Roots in the Skies

Madagascar

Last night I dreamed of a planet

Where more hides than can ever be seen

Where shy creatures that sing to the
    sunrise

Play touch-tag in a forest of green

Last night I dreamed of a highway

Dry dusty with zebus and flies

Where small children who wear rags as
    raiment

Play sad clowns beneath roots in the skies

Last night I dreamed of an island

Where the language unspoken is blue

Then this morning I woke to discover

That all I had dreamed of was true

He Lived Among Us

Tribute to Nelson Mandela (1918-2013)

He lived among us –
This child named Rolihlahla
This boy called Nelson
This man we knew as Mandela –
And now he is gone

He shared our days –
This son of Africa, our Madiba
This father of a nation, our Tata
This guardian of humanity, our Elder –
And now he is gone

He was one of us –
This shepherd of the people
This harbinger of hope and joy
This legend of our time and place –
And now he is gone

He was our leader
Our defender, our nation's spear
And he showed us how to fight

He was our enemy
Our nemesis, our conscience
And he showed us how to be free

He was our light
Our sun, our inspiration
And he showed us how to forgive

Yet did we ever really know him?
This lawyer who became an outlaw
This soldier who became a peacemaker
This prisoner who became a liberator

How can we fathom his depths?
This father who lost a son and wife
This comrade who lost so many friends
This martyr who lost twenty-seven years

How can we see into his heart?
This intellectual who became an activist
This statesman who became a gardener
This icon who became the world's beloved

We remember him
For his skilful manoeuvring
Through the political maze
And even more for his love of dancing

We remember him
For his human touch
Among the powerful and the powerless
And even more for his love of children

We remember him
For his failures and foibles
That made him fallible like us
And even more for his love of justice

He lived among us –
And now it is for us to carry his torch
        onward

It is for us to follow his shining example

It is for us to fight for his unshakeable
ideals –

Now that he is gone

He shared our days –

And now we must make the rest of our days
count

We must work as he did to set others free

We must show that the spirit can triumph
in the end –

Now that he is gone

He was one of us –

And now we are challenged to become one
of him

We are inspired to be the best we can be

We are reminded that I am because we
are –

Now that he is gone

Nkosi Sikelel' iMandela!

We will honour his memory

By never losing faith in times of adversity
We will celebrate his life
By always daring to hope for a miracle
We will keep his legacy alive
By choosing to walk daily in his footsteps
On the path of love
Amandla! Awethu!

Land of Emerald Dreams

Swellendam, South Africa

Low clouds of grey left far behind
Exchanged for open skies of blue
Black asphalt trails and dusty fields
Give way to scenes of verdant hue

Beneath the mountain's misty brow
Beneath the oak trees' dappled shade
A canvass for the nomad's brush
A staging post for passing trade

Drink in the cool of whitewashed walls
Drift off to cricket symphonies
Breathe deep the scent of sun-bleached
    thatch
Awake to birdsong melodies

Past craggy cliffs of rusty shards
Through hidden tracks of forest greens
Refreshed by waterfall cascades
Behold the land of emerald dreams

Thirty Five

Thirty five and still alive
Learning all over how to survive
Looking all over for my lost drive
Hoping in time again I'll thrive

Maybe 2006 will bring a fix
A chance to learn new tricks
To find something that clicks
By the time I'm thirty six

Poem for New Year

The year is new
Poised
And expectant:

Like a spring coiled and ready to be sprung
Or a tangled ball of wool, come undone
Like a gleaming highway slick for smooth
      travel
Or a dusty footpath strewn with rough
      gravel

Poised
And expectant
The year is new:

Like a newborn lamb unsteady on its legs
Or a stale pot of coffee brewed from the
      dregs
Like stepping forward, each step like the
      last
Or leaping the nest, escaping the past

Poised
The year is new
And expectant:

Like a see-sawing scale, about to tip
Or a teetering cliff, afraid to slip
Like a snail slid across a line in the sand
Or the long thin finger of destiny's hand

The year is new
Poised
And expectant

I Wish She'd Stayed

In Memoriam: Karen Weinberg

She made me laugh – let's start with that
(The time she wore a witches' hat)
Her cheeky banter full of fun
And, on my word, she loved to pun

Enthralled by British comedies
From Eddie Izzard to John Cleese
Held captive by Austen's tease
(Young Darcy jellified her knees)

And then there was that Stephen Fry
(She'd have proposed, but she was shy)
True, he is gay, but love is blind
And she was smitten with his mind

She lived for art and loved to sing
Such colours in her offering
The shadow of Matopos stones
The glow of rusty vineyard tones

Baryshnikov upon the wall
Unfettered horses in the hall
She saw the beauty, heard its tune
She caught the light, lassoed the moon

King Singers' a capella hums
Dusty stomps of tribal drums
Her world aloft on violin strains
Juluka flowing in her veins

Soprano voices in the air
Mama Mia's songs of cheer
The concert halls, the silver screen
She soared the heights, touched the dream

Her head was swirled with maths and stars
Her memories stitched with faded scars
She knew the dark, yet channelled light
She felt earthbound, yet showed us flight

She long ago left creed behind
And saw all faiths as intertwined

Her wisdom caught the ebb and flow
Of New Age waves and Oprah's show

So deeply loved, and yet alone
She found her peace, her bay view home
Her friends and loved ones scattered wide
She was the rock, we were the tide

Just like a snowflake's crystal maze
Her beauty sparkled through our days
And just as ice must melt and flow
Back to the source – we must let go

Our daughter, teacher, friend and sister
How we loved her, how we miss her
We will not let her vision fade
Now she is gone – I wish she'd stayed

Grief

I have no way to know your grief
No salve of rhyme to bring relief
No words of wisdom or belief
No way to cheat life's senseless thief

I have no way to block the pain
No shelter from the driving rain
No words to make the madness sane
No way to dry what tears remain

I have no light for these dark days
No shining star or warm sun's rays
No passage through the lonely maze
No honey for death's bitter ways

Yet with these simple words I send
My love and blessings as a friend
With hope that broken hearts can mend
And faith that this is not the end

Gorky Park

Moscow, Russia

A summer day in Gorky Park
The world is freshly green and bright
New lovers stroll and children lark
While bladers glide in happy flight

A sky of grey, a wrung-out heart
My world is teetered on a knife
I wander, silent and apart
While shadows stalk my happy life

The Barefoot Don

Tribute to Manfred Max-Neef

He walks the mountains, plains and fields
At home with forests, wolves and birds
He's naked in the power he wields:
The sword of truth; the axe of words

He knows the chill of foreign lands
And sighs the loss of good friends passed
He feels the warmth of welcome hands
And beams the joy of love that lasts

He's felt the ire of dictators
And known the grace of humble kings
He's filled up books and newspapers
And given gifts of voice and wings

He warns of theories, now unmasked
That leave the earth and people cursed
He points the way – we all are tasked
With putting needs and nature first

He says to see, just close your eyes
To hear, be still and feel your heart
Real changes always wear disguise
And grassroots play a hidden part

Then in the quiet hours between
He listens to the tides of Brahms
Or pens and plays a piece he's dreamed
Or rests within his lover's arms

He's just a barefoot 'household' don
Whose feet have trod the sacred round
He counts success by hearts he's won
And handshakes from the underground

Postscript:

Dear Manfred, if you read this ode
You'll know the gratitude I feel
For our chance meeting on the road
And spokes of friendship on life's wheel

Thirty Six

I am thirty six
And in one long short year
My world has changed
Expanded
Intensified
With more shades
Of dark and light

I have ascended to summits of hope
And tunnelled through caves of despair
Without giving up

I have skipped across meadows of ecstasy
And waded in swamps of sadness
Without being trapped

I have showered under waterfalls of passion
And walked on glaciers of numbness
Without losing heart

I have strolled on beaches of contentment
And battled with tides of disappointment
Without being drowned

Each frontier I cross
Expands my awareness
And deepens my understanding

Each horizon I chase
Widens my experience
And heightens my sensitivity

Each new low I plumb
Lowers my expectations
And raises my beliefs

Each new high I scale
Softens my defences
And hardens my resolve

I am tired
And yet I feel that my reserves

Are being steadily replenished

I am adrift
And yet I sense that the wind
Is blowing in the right direction

I am alone
And yet I seem to be starting
To open my heart to possibility

I am scarred
And yet I am a little more prepared
To contemplate trusting again

I no longer brush away my tears
For they help me to smile
With my eyes

I no longer curse the darkness
For it helps me to pay attention
To the light

I no longer fear the pain

For it helps me to know beauty

More intensely

I no longer hide from uncertainty

For it helps me to cherish moments

Of knowing clarity

I am thirty six

And I have emerged

From the cocoon of self-pity

Bewildered

Relieved

With wings

Still wet and crumpled

Genesis Islands

Galapagos, Ecuador

Genesis islands, straddling Hades and
    Eden
Ancient follies forged in the fiery mists of
    time
Land of contortion between struggle and
    freedom
An ode to creation and its ebb-flowing
    rhyme

Puzzle of the Pacific, of cold blood and fire
A cauldron of species, our map of history
Giant tortoises tread with evolution's desire
Our past leaves a trail, our future a mystery

Saludo! To Darwin and his unholy treason

Marie's Poem

Written for Marie Steyn

I know a special lady
And you may know her too
She's just so vriendelik
What's a guy to do!

I know a gentle lady
She is a Kaapse nooi
I would not tell a lie
Sy's so vreeslik mooi!

I know a clever lady
She has great taste in men
You ask me how I know?
I am one of them!

I know a lekker lady
She always makes me smile
She tells such rude grappe
With consummate style!

I know a super lady
She doesn't mince her words
She'll say just what she thinks:
'Jong! That's for the birds!'

I know a loving lady
She cares from start to end
What's more, kan jy dit glo?
Sy's my beste friend

The End

In the end

Life is cruel

It takes

Too much

Too soon

It gives

Too little

Too late.

Do not

Be fooled

Every ending

Is not

A new beginning

Some endings

Are just

The end.

Life is cruel

In the end

It cuts

Too deep

Too quick

It hurts

Too much

Too long.

Still

It is true

Every ending

Had a bright beginning

And a middle

Rich

With meaning

To the end.

Life is cruel

In the end

It tears

All apart

All away

It grinds

All before
All to dust.

All we can do
Is celebrate
The beginning
Cherish
The middle
And live
Fully
To the end.

The Dragon and the Phoenix

China

You are the mighty dragon
Whose history is lost in the mists of time
Shrouded in mystery and enchantment
And breathing fire

Your dragon emperors
Ruled the endless skies and earth
With flaming tongue and snaking tail
And armoured scales

The dragon flies again
Awaking from its night of red dreams
Craving the horded treasures of the West
And rising like a golden sun

Waxing like a silver moon
Shining the ancient wisdom of the East
Trailing iridescent sparks of change
The phoenix flies again

Cocooned in silk
And flowing with ripples of water
Through peaceful rockeries and gardens
Were your phoenix empresses

Singing spells
And rising in a blaze of coloured feathers
From the ashes of grey modernity
You are the mystical phoenix

Thirty Seven

This moment is marked on my journey of
    days

As I wander the forest of shadowy ways

With my feet on the path in the moon-
    dappled light

And my eyes on the stars in the cloud-
    blotted night

The treasure I found in this buried year's
    chest

Was the knowledge I gained from
    philosophy's quest

Which was further enriched by my travels
    from home

To the wilderness delta and temples of
    stone

The story untold is of dreams to fulfil

Of my life as an artist with parchment and
    quill

By the light of the candle of love in my
    heart

And the call of adventure to make a new start

This Day

*Commemorating Barack Obama's 2009
Inauguration as United States
President*

This day

Is not just any day

It is a day of days

A day of a lifetime

An epoch making day

At a time that cries out

For new beginnings

This day

Is a watershed day

A day that separates

Yesterday from today

And today from tomorrow

On a mindless march of days

That needed breaking

This day

Is a day to be marked

As something remarkable

A day to be celebrated

As something joyful

A day to be remembered

As something historic

This day

Is a tribute to the past

With its sacrifices of so many

A blessing for the present

Amidst looming clouds of despair

And a vision for the future

Welcomed with an open hand

This day

Is not the struggle's end

But the journey's beginning

It is not the death of prejudice

But the life of possibility

It is not the end of nights

But the start of days

This day
Is not so much a forging ahead
As a long overdue catching up
With changes at last
That begin to give life
To time-honoured ideals
And flickering hopes

This day
Is a day of coming together
When power meets responsibility
And rhetoric meets action
It is a day of empowerment
When the voiceless are heard
And the marginal become mainstream

This day
Is a day of reconciliation
When the past is laid to rest
And the future is awakening

It is a day of prodigals
When the lost find their way home
And a nation rejoins the world

Lasso Poet

Written About Wendy Cope

I've met a poet or two
While tucked under the covers
Or soaking in the tub
With bubble dreams of lovers

And sometimes in the park
I've heard them softly giggle
Or fumbling in the dark
I've felt their word-worms wriggle

But giddy-gum delight
Watch me do a jiggly jive
Upon this hum-drum night
I met a poet still alive!

Her famous biting wit
With which she's known to poke
Is wicked when it's writ
But wickeder when spoke

Some say that she's besotted

Her words are strung like rope

But whether straight or knotted

You're bound to like Ms Cope

Cove of the Caspian

Baku, Azerbaijan

The scattered seeds of history
Lie buried in the desert shade
And watered by the crescent moon
Rise up to form a sickle blade

Minarets and sacred domes
Caravans and loving homes
Maiden towers, rising blocks
Tireless cranes and bustling docks

The past now seems a distant shore
The present rides an oil-slick tide
And as the trade winds bluff and blow
The city chugs and churns with pride

Thirty Eight

A lifetime lived in just one year
At least that's how it seems to me
And what began with clouds of fear
Now ends in luminosity
I would not call it chance or fate
I simply call it thirty eight

I travelled into dragon's lairs
To fairest capes and cactus plains
I visited the land of bears
And markets hid in dusty lanes
I saw creation, small and great
I roamed the globe to thirty eight

In matters of the heart I found
That like a drum with changing beat
I had to find my solid ground
Before I danced with happy feet
I cannot say the road's been straight
I wound my way to thirty eight

The call of words was ever strong
The poet-scholar dipped his quill
The flow of ink was short and long
The script an act of wisp and will
I say to live is to create
I know it's true at thirty eight

The dusk of winter brings goodbyes
As I prepare to take my leave
From gilded halls and lofty spires
To conjure up fresh city dreams
I know that it is not too late
I start again at thirty eight

Renaissance Man

Tribute to Leonardo Da Vinci

Born on a Saturday, third hour of night

With Tuscan hills bathed in the star
      spangled light

Ser Piero's great pride and Vinci's great joy

He was Chaterina's illegitimate boy

At sixteen, he followed the Arno's swift flow

And joined as apprentice to Verrocchio

To learn to perfect the painter's high trade

Of capturing light and harnessing shade

He started by painting a tranquil glade
      scene,

Then the Madonnas and the pose of Benci,

The Magi adored, the penitent Saint –

All brought back to life on his canvass with
      paint

At thirty he travelled to the city Milano

An envoy in chief for the ruler Lorenzo

He was sent to the court of his patron il
      Moro
To give him a glimpse through the veil of
      tomorrow

In a letter, he made his offer prodigious –
From building of weapons to laying of
      bridges
Even a lyre from a horse-skull and strings –
In his words: "An infinite variety of things"

For seventeen years he stayed in that
      quarter
Designing new ways to regulate water
While filling his days with Paragone theses
Of legends and myths and fantasy species

At Paradise Feast, the heavens displayed
With magical motion effects that he made;
And a three-tier city was part of his plan,
As was his great wheel of Vetruvius man

He pictured the Virgin on bleak rocky shore

And captured an artist with his music
score,

Then Cecelia posing with snow-white
ermine,

Before re-enacting the last supper scene

His equine colossus was sculpted from clay

His Platonic drawings on published display

His thoughts and ideas in codexes bound

His paintings commissioned to bless holy
ground

From Mantua to Venice, from Florence to
Rome

Montefeltro to Paris - all made them his
home;

From Leo the Tenth to Louis the First -

They all were enchanted by his mental
thirst

As architect, engineer, artist and sage

Biologist, scientist ahead of his age

Inventor of unbelievable things

An unsurpassed genius, this legend of
wings

He towers above the landscape of time

With brilliant ideas and visions sublime

Still no one can fathom the depths of his
guile

Or unlock the secret of Mona's half smile

And even though five hundred years have
gone by

He calls us to stretch out our mind-wings
and fly

To join in the journey that he once began

And walk in the steps of the Renaissance
Man.

A Promise of New Worlds

The journeys we plan
The trips we make
The holidays we remember –
All are vivid fantasies
Conjured from desire
Unattainable utopias
Wished upon a dream
Sun-picked memories
Pocketed for a rainy day

Travel itself is a shoddy garment
Creased with frumpled fatigue
And stained by leaky plans

Travel is a soundtrack of static hiss
For a fleeting moment of silence
Or a passing parade of trumpets

Travel is an ill begotten escape
Which tunnels back on itself
To the familiar prison of our thoughts

And yet a jacket well worn
Gives a certain comfort
And tells a story of its own
The flash of blinding wellbeing
And the flood of sensual bliss
Make the dissonance worthwhile
And ultimately, travel delivers its promise
Taking us to new, undiscovered worlds
But never the ones we expected

Gone Too Soon

In Memoriam: Margaret Legum

Like a raven in the night
You've taken flight
Taken flight
Towards the light

Like a sliver of the moon
You're gone too soon
Gone too soon
With one last swoon

Like a current in the stream
You're flowing free
Flowing free
Towards the sea

Like the whisper of a sigh
You've bid goodbye
Bid goodbye
With one last why

Like a rainbow in the mist

You're dearly missed

Dearly missed

Forever missed

Loss

It is loss
(As much as gain)
That binds us

It is pain
(As much as joy)
That joins us

It is suffering
(As much as satisfaction)
That moulds us

It is darkness
(As much as light)
That defines us

It is death
(As much as life)
That tests us

It is regret
(As much as foresight)
That bends us

It is rest
(As much as effort)
That sustains us

It is loss
(As much as love)
That makes us

Thirty Nine

As markets crashed and wild fires spread
Fresh waves of doubt splashed in my head
So seas of promise turned to sands
And snuffed the flame of future plans

Then darkness warmed to fragile day
My scattered ruins left on display
And though rebuilding had begun
It took some time to find the sun

Now as the year draws to a close
The icy water melts and flows
I cut the rope and trust to time
Upon the ocean thirty nine

A Tale of Two Cities

Mannheim, Germany

A modern city by the river –
The brochure purred enticingly
Omitting to mention
That it was flattened in the war
Then rebuilt as a lego-block town
Cut off from the river
By a ten track railway

Blessed with blue skies and sunshine –
My photos will nod in silent assent
Without ever showing
That my feet were aching
From walking in worn out shoes
Through a maze of dead-ends
To reach the elusive river

Against the backdrop of an elegant bridge –
My pictures will show a windswept smile
But stay mute, deaf and blind

To the jackhammer rattle
Clattering on the icy breeze
From across the busy channel

With a perfect promenade for lovers –
I will recall the cosy, strolling couples
But conveniently forget
That my mind was far away
Wondering what she was doing
And wishing she was here
Or I was there, back home

And yet there is a hidden city that lingers –
The unspoken sights
Of dancing fountains and pansy blooms
The invisible sounds
Of youthful buzz and ancient whispers
These are the unexpected discoveries
Which, once revealed
Turn shadow promises into authentic
        delights

Dream-Shaper

Tribute to Antoni Gaudí

The very first glance took my breath away

Turning hungry night into thirsty day

With explosions of riotous colour

And swirling ideas like no other

With stone and glass curving

And wood fronds unfurling

On rooftops with teardrops

And courtyards with light-shards

You crashed in waves on my empty shore

And shook the caves of my hollow core

You stir the memory of ancient trees

And rouse the longing for restless seas

You bend and refract

My courage to act

To sculpt and create

My fusions of fate

You round my sharp edges

And speak my soul's pledges

To fill my life's ocean
With colour and motion

Your great gleaming spires
Hang suspended like wires
Between heaven and earth
Between magic and mirth
They echo creation
And spark revelation
To break with convention
And live with intention
To be builder and breaker
To become a dream-shaper

Tide of White

Edinburgh, Scotland

The tide of white
The peaceful fight
Coming, ready or not
Lest Africa's forgot
Coming to the shores
Of the Scottish moors
Knocking on the doors
Of the fortress eight
Questioning the laws
Of the Third World's fate
From dissatisfaction
Comes a call to action
On debt and aid
And fair world trade

The snaking convoy
The voiceless envoy
Converging on the Meadows
Merging in the shadows

The masses flock
In patient gridlock
To start the march
With banners arched
Then the final crush
Before the rush
Circling the city
With hope, not pity
The tide of white
To make wrongs right

Forty

What a year! Oh, what a year!
Around the block, around the bend
Around the world and back again
In time for snow and Christmas cheer!

What I've seen! Oh, what I've seen!
The fire's strong, the fire's bright
I chased the sun, I braved the night
I woke the muse and lived the dream!

What a time! Oh, what a time!
Of meeting minds, of meeting fears
Of random walks and World Cup cheers
I searched for reason, found my rhyme!

What a find! Oh, what a find!
To look beyond, to look within
To see a place I could begin
To leave the phantom past behind!

What a day! Oh, what a day!
When snowflakes danced with naked trees
When moonboats sailed on tranquil seas
Our dreams were young and love at play!

What a joy! Oh, what a joy!
To be so loved, to be so blessed
To still be on life's sacred quest
I'm all grown up, yet still a boy!

What a life! What paths I tread!
Through valleys low, to mountain peaks
With flowing words through hidden creeks
I'm forty, with the best ahead!

Shining

Tribute to Hugh Masekela

smooth
silky sounds
shuffling and sliding
shape-shifting and slipping
snaking along the velvet air
this music raw and rare
tribute to a legend
the maestro, the one and the only
the Trumpet Lonely
Hugh Masekela
his spirit rebounding
his echo resounding:
bring back Nelson Mandela
back Nelson Mandela
Nelson Mandela
Mandela
...
and tonight
under the pulsing light

he's poised like a cobra
swaying before striking
mesmerising
hypnotising
moving from the shadows
grooving in the echoes
as the music tip-toes
on and on and on it goes
before tripping and flipping
and beat-stripping into
foot tap-tap-tapping and
knee slap-slapping and
hand clapping
music in motion
momentum mounting
swirling eddies in a stream
stoked coals glowing
perspiration showing
steadily building up steam
like a locomotive
a-hissing and a-huffing
and a-plodding and a-puffing

and a chugging and a-chuffing

stimela! a-hamba!

shosholoza

shhhhhhh!

...

toot-tooooooooot!

go train go!

go slow, go steady

gather up steam, get ready

for the steep mountain climb

the syncopated time

the synchronised rhythm of rhyme

overlaid and understated

overplayed and underrated

the song talk

the long walk to freedom

we won't forget

we'll never regret

the way we won

the day the sun

came shining

the people lining

the suburbs and the streets

the colours and the beats

no we won't forget

the day the sun

came shining

shining

the sun, the day

the way we came

together

as one

shining

Eternal City

Rome, Italy

Soak up
With all your senses
The Eternal City:

Ancient playground of gods
Fertile seedbed of legends
Feared seat of empire-builders
Gore-stained arena of gladiators
Dusty parade of soldiers
Muse-filled gallery of artists
Colourful canvass of architects
Taste parlour of connoisseurs
Intoxicating goblet of wine
Floodlit stage of sports-heroes
Nectar trap for tourists
Living history-book of people

Tell Me Your Story

Written for Jeanette Hilda Visser (Mom)

Tell me your story – I am here listening:
About higher souls and chosen roles
And learning lessons since your birth;
About taking part in life's great art
And bringing healing to the earth.

Tell me your story: I want to know all
About swarming bees and chimpanzees
And throwing stones for your pet dog;
About dairy rounds and farmyard sounds
And fairies inside hollow logs.

Tell me your story: I want to know all
About love affairs and riding mares
And shooting trophies that you won;
About teenage flights and party nights
And meeting *him* – that special one.

Tell me your story: I want to know all
About wedding bells and baby spells
And building your own house of dreams;
About paddling days and bush-war frays
And learning what true friendship means.

Tell me your story: I want to know all
About taking stands and moving lands
And starting over once again;
About camping trips and scouting tips
And growing esoteric ken.

Tell me your story: I want to know all
About hiking trails and mother's tales
And children growing up too soon;
About wedded hands and shifting sands
And dancing to the Nana tune.

Tell me your story: I want to know all
About crossing seas and great oak trees
And feeling that you had come home;

About gardens green and countries seen
And shedding light where're you roam.

Tell me your story – I am listening still:
About loved ones lost and heartache's cost
And moments filled with joy as well;
About living true and being you –
There's such a story left to tell!

Forty One

Another bumpy trip around the chunky
      sun

With far less battles lost than new victories
      won

I'm far from my old age and yet no longer
      young

I've only just got started – I'm firing forty
      one

Another funky flip inside my clunky head

With fewer fears to face, yet ever skins to
      shed

I'm eager to find out what paths still lay
      ahead

I'm keeping my feet light wherever I may
      tread

Another chunky chip in my life's hunky
      dough

With far less cause to shrink and much
      more chance to grow

I'm ready to become the star of my own
   show

I'm sailing on the wind and surfing in the
   flow

Another monkey trick of clockwork flunky
   fun

With no less time to waste and such great
   love to come

I'm gazing at the stars with dreams still left
   to run

I've only just got started – I'm firing forty
   one

Transatlantic Pilgrims

California, Arizona & Nevada, USA

I. Pilgrims

We set out for adventure
In the fabled land of the free
Where the eagle rules the skies
And the bear roams the forests

We are transatlantic pilgrims
Come to this brave new world
To walk ancient paths
In search of natural wonders

II. Expectations

We take our first steps
In a myth-laden landscape
Dreamed into being
By hallucinations of history and hearsay

We strain our ears listening

For lyrical echoes of sunshine and
    revolution

We scan the horizon looking

For glorious valleys of silicon and wine

III. Arrival

Our idyllic bubble quickly bursts

As we are spat out

From the airport's shiny cocoon

Onto tangled spaghetti highways

We pass beneath the shadow

Of sprawling industrial scree

And hungry grey asphalt plains

Below thirsty brown slopes

IV. In Transit

The beacons to our hotel

Are garish neon fast-food signs

Demarcating a red-light district
Of gaudy commercial prostitution

Underwhelmed by first impressions
Sedated by jetlag and traffic lullabies
In our drab-camouflaged cell block
Sleep tests our faith in dreams

V. San Francisco

Downtown rescues our shaken dreams
Rocked in the cradle of its blue crescent
      bay
Invigorated by the breath of its green lungs
Uplifted by the colours of its rainbow flag

The city's arched back bristles with
      concrete
As cable cars claw their way up deja-vu
      hills
Bridge arms and quay fingers reach out
To its caged island heart of stone

VI. Tahoe

Near the rim of the world

Leopard-spotted hills and snake-winding
     roads

Accompany the lilt of Rocky Mountain High

And inspire crisp-aired alpine aspirations

The lake reflects a utopian vision

Of people carving out wholesome lives

Sensitive to the animation of trees

And the living presence of ancestors

VII. Yosemite

Possessed by the spirit of Moses

We gaze in awe at the cloven landscape

Enchanted by the crevasse-cracked horizon

Our faith in miracles restored

Diminutive beneath towering edifices of
     granite

Silent before thundering cliffs of water

Our passage through these elongated vistas
Shrinks our ego and stretches our soul

VIII. Waterfalls

In the distance we glimpse her shadowed
    face
With windswept hair cascading wildly
Her viridescent gown shapely pregnant
Her cool wet feet wriggling and toes
    trickling

We wend our way past bubbling cauldrons
Through thrashing splashing roaring
    ravines
Climbing ladders of stone and rungs of mist
To reach the tumultuous quenching source

IX. Sequoias

Worship comes naturally
Amidst the cathedral pillars and celestial
    spires

Of these millennial sentinels

Who serve as rope ladders for the gods

With elephantine feet, gnarled toes and
    charred ankles

Bulbous joints, fibrous skin and tufted
    heads

These gargantuan elders

Are the sacred guardians of earth's history

X. Los Angeles

The home of the stars shines only in the
    dark

Invention laboratory of smog and gridlock

This is where vanities are pumped up

And overexposed holograms hide

Beneath the enigmatic Hollywood sign

Master illusionists weave magic for the
    world

While their puppets submit to green
    incarceration

Under the spell of misplaced heroism

XI. Trees

Elastic trees stretch ever skyward

Roots wrestling for cool slaking tonic

Limbs sparring for ethereal radiant nectar

Plotting their escape from darkness into
    light

Supple saplings sprout eagerly

Sturdy giants endure patiently

Fallen comrades feed the living

Forests are the book of life

XII. Las Vegas

A luminescent oasis in the desert of
    blandness

The impersonation capital of the world

Draws hopefuls like a moth to a flame
Blinded by the harsh light of materialism

Yet beneath its gimcrack plastic veneer
Imagination and artistry give shape
To untold possibilities of creation
Unshackled by chains of gold

XIII. Grand Canyon

Stepping through the doors of time
Descending the stairs of history
We find ourselves in a colossal gallery
Displaying Nature's priceless masterpieces

Spilled palettes streak the rocky canvass
Sculpted steeples mark a halloed
    installation
Erosion-carved veins course brown and
    green
While ageless etched red faces look on
    wisely

XIV. Flight

Nimble bats and iridescent jays
Acrobatic swifts and circling raptors
Silhouetted gulls and ski-landing ducks
Our wish to fly is why we speak of heaven

As our shiny metal bird takes to the skies
Although our pilgrimage is at an end
We are forever uplifted
On the wings of our California dreaming

Good to Say Goodbye

It's good to say goodbye -

When you know that it's not forever

When you believe that the journey is just
  begun

When the farewell is full of love

It's good to say goodbye -

When the way behind is a long, proud trail

When the path has become, of late, too
  steep

When the way ahead is lighter

It's good to say goodbye -

When the parting brings relief

When companions are ready to go their own
  way

When now is the right time

It's good to say goodbye -

When death seeds new life

When exit from one world is entry to
    another

When sorrow mingles with a smile

Stranger

How strange to knock upon the door

Of a place I'd known long years before

To be welcomed in by friends estranged

See familiar furniture rearranged

To wander the maze of old memory halls

To listen to echoes of distant recalls

To search for the signs where the past left
its print

Of my passage through time, some small
clue or a hint

But the harder I looked, the more seemed
the same

'Til it finally became clear, it was I who had
changed

Forty Two

It was the year
That rocked with the shock
Of the stopping clock
That choked with the smoke
Of the hearts that broke
That bled on the edge
Of the reaper's wedge

And so the dark endings
Became painful bendings
In the path to slow mending

It was the year
That burst with the thirst
For creation's first
That spawned with the form
Of a chrysalis born
That gleamed with the beam
Of a kaleidoscope meme

And so the winged swarmings

Became hopeful dawnings

To new ways of performing

It was the year

That was blighted and slighted

Yet still over-flighted

That was spanned over grand

And exotic lands

That I grew as I flew

And chased after the blue

And now the fresh dew

Of beginning anew

In the year forty two

The Highwaymen

I catch glimpses of them sometimes - the
shadow people:

Peering wearily from their highway hideouts

Almost invisible behind their camouflage
cladding

Of earth-stained rags, litter-lego shelters
and unwanted persons status

They strike fear into the hearts of many -
these desperados:

Preying on the numb conscience of society

Having nothing, they have nothing to lose

In their battle for survival on the fringes of
existence

I wonder how dangerous they are - the
bridge stowaways:

Watching the rushing world go by, to and
fro

Living from land to hand to bottle to mouth

In a cycle of semi-conscious passive
resistance

Their freedom threatens to make us less
free - these fugitives:

Running from the iron hand of the law of
economics

Hiding to escape the cruel prison of forced
daily labour

Of those trapped in motor car coffins and
office block cells

They are thieves of the most tragic kind -
the highwaymen:

Assaulting our sense of justice, of right and
wrong

Stripping our moral fibre and robbing our
dignity

In a society that is meant to care for its
weakest and most vulnerable

Nexus

Johannesburg, South Africa

Scattered rays of light converge
Rainbow people meet and merge
Upon the stage of Jozi town
Something big is going down

Colours clash and swirl and spark
Dancing flames light up the dark
Of narrow minds and vested veils
Of widening gaps and toppled scales

The world will never be the same
What's lost is mourned, yet much is gained
Our hearts unite with beating drum
And spirits rise as hopes are sung

I See You Clearly

In Memoriam: Bob Steyn

I see you clearly -

Framed with humble grey suit

Centred with flaming chalice tie

Irreverent with peeping red socks

I see you clearly -

Furrowed frown echoing with emotion

Bristling brows dancing with animation

Crinklecut curls waving with wildness

I see you clearly -

Hunched in embracing conversation

Pursed in loving greeting

Drawing in smoky pleasure

I see you clearly -

Cradling a bewildered baby

Signing a watery cross

Affirming a yes to life

I see you clearly -

Extended arms in wide welcome

Cradling hands joining a nervous pair

Poetic voice invoking the prophet

I see you clearly -

Hands interwoven in sad prayer

Head bowed in painful remembering

Eyes consoling in enduring hope

I see you clearly -

Eyes tired with demands of work

Face lined with sorrow of others in need

Shoulders stooped with sickness of the
      world

I see you clearly -

Step light upon leafy mountain track

Being engaged among scholarly stones

Smile wide amidst bubbles of community

I see you clearly -

Embraced by bursting books ceiling high

Perched upon tiny stool in listening pose

Writing at huddled desk icon blessed

I see you clearly -

Gazing deeply into her eyes

Gently alighting a butterfly kiss

Beaming a love that makes you whole

I see you clearly -

Not only in cherished memories

But animated in living imagination

Independent of time and space

I see you clearly -

Engaging me in platonic dialogue as you
     teach me

Winking encouragement or raising
     eyebrows as you watch over me

Tugging and stretching the very canvass of
     my reality as you beckon to me

Empty Spaces

Empty spaces
Left behind
Silent paces
Without rhyme
Painful traces
To remind
Fading faces
Over time
Woven laces
Now unwind
Nothing replaces
Love sublime
Empty spaces
So unkind

Forty Three

It was the year of Bordeaux cheese fondue
And St Emilion's catacomb
Of steaming springs in Montagu
And cold Cape ocean tides of blue

There was Zurich's placid lake
And Copenhagen's mermaid muse
Paris streets and Seoul's bright lights
And Corfu's glistening turquoise hue

It was the year of Moscow's Gorky Park
And Dexter's secrets in the dark
Of Botero's ark in Bogota
And the Petrol Christ in Barranca

There was Murano's rainbow glass
And Burano's colourful scenes
Da Vinci's feats and Venchi's delight
And gondola canals to emerald dreams

It was the year of scholars' gowns
And triumph through the ups and downs
Of butterflies from the cocoon
And fireflies beneath the moon

There was Gothenburg's white wonderland
And Bangalore's 'Horn OK Please'
Mandela's long walk ended, now he's free
This was the year of forty three

The Day the World Changed

New York, USA

One fateful hour of horror!
And the smug safety of every shore
is shattered
The waves of live media-feeds
come crashing in
Smashing our fragile senses
with hyper-dramatic images
Dashing our turbulent emotions
against the rocks of a new reality

Symbols of the free world tumble!
At the earthquake's epicentre
    of death and destruction
Leaving nations shaking and shuddering
    with rage and fear
Left to search through the rubble and ruins
    where towers of pride once stood
Hoping for a miraculous rescue
    of their beliefs and way of life

The world holds its breath!
As the toll of tragic loss ticks
    like a time bomb
Of grief and mourning and depression
    and hatred and revenge
Some desperately looking for ways
to contain the blast
Others scanning the horizon for a target
    on which to explode

The war against terrorism begins!
With a campaign for the ritual slaughter
of a scape goat
And a defiant display of frustrated firepower
    and propaganda sorties
Leaving in its wake a cratered moonscape
    of humanitarian crises
And a minefield of cultural and religious
    tensions
    that lie unexploded

The world has changed forever!

Forcing us to venture beyond the fortress

    of our comfortable self-indulgence

Prompting us to dig deeper than the
    shallow well

    of our cultural arrogance

Pleading with us to rise up out of the
    morass

    of our religious intolerance

Helping, in our quest for meaning, to realise

that the enemy is within

Love and Blessings

Love and blessings on this day
The long dark night
Has warmed to light
The sun's rays shine
And church bells chime
To tell the world the happy news

Love and blessings on this day
The sky is blue
Life's made anew
This summer morn
A baby's born
All nature smiles to celebrate

Love and blessings on this day
The hopes and fears
The laughs and tears
All end in joy
A precious boy
Welcome to your life on earth

Love and blessings on this day

The baby's cries

Are met with sighs

The parents' eyes

Are filled with pride

Loved ones gather close around

Love and blessings on this day

Wee tiny toes

And cutest nose

Sweet hands and face

All's in its place

A perfect little human being

Love and blessings on this day

So many care

Who can't be there

They send their wishes

Hugs and kisses

Rest easy now in their embrace

Love and blessings on this day

Flowers bloom

Just like the moon

And each new dawn

The world's reborn

The circle of life's begun anew

A Place to Bury Your Heart

Romania

The towering city tumbles easily into village
and field

Exchanging its coat of grey for a tunic of
green

The snaking road entwines river and
railway

Past oil wells tirelessly flexing their
mechanical muscles

And corn farms harvesting their crop of
human toil

Monsters of industry loom like shadows
from a bygone era

Devouring and digesting resources

Breathing in energy and exhaling clouds of
poison

And by a tantalising trick of technology

Spitting out trinkets of modern convenience

Savage cliffs embrace the panoramic
skyline

Like geological petals unfolding

Revealing forests of waving green and gold

An intoxicating pollen of purity

To the hungry gatherers of Nature's
inspiration

The Heroes' Cross stands like a solitary
sentinel

Keeping watch over the battlefield of life

Bittersweet history echoes down the
passages of time

In castles, cathedrals and haunted prison
cells of memory

Tombstones to the sacrifices of the many
for the few

The patterns of the past are danced into the
present

In whirling spray of colour and song

While the present is sown into the promise
of the future

With magic seeds of friendship and trust
A fertile land - a place to bury your heart

Gran

Written for Jessie Foster

My memories of childhood drift

Like lazy clouds across a blue African sky

Their phantom shapes not quite
    discernable

Their misty emotions forever changing

Storm clouds are rare among them -

Fleeting electric flashes of self-indulgent
    anger

Dull, distant thunder-rolls of disturbing
    fear

Most are wispy, white, feather clouds -

Good-weather scripts of promise and
    confidence

Magnetic spray patterns of compelling
    destiny

Some are fluffy cotton wool clouds -

Comforting blankets of cosy support

Wrapped around in a warm joyful embrace
...
Like my memories of you, Gran

I remember silver pots of steaming weak tea

And feeding fat earthworms in the mulch
    patch

And tracking giant Matabele ants in the
    scorching dust

I remember yummy picnics in the park

And fishing fever at the dam

And trips to the mystical Matopos to gaze
    from God's window

I remember playful yapping dogs

And sweet spoils from Meikles

And exciting excursions to Eskimo Hut

I remember thrilling pulsing electrical
    storms

And intoxicating raindrops on parched
    bush

And scented carpets of lilac Jacaranda

I remember magical sooty overnight train
  rides

And roadside treasure hunts for carvings

And awesome encounters with elephant
  elders

I remember your caring inquisitive way

With random strangers on beaches and
  benches

And you, resplendent in green, at our
  wedding celebration

I remember always your welcome lap

And your tinkling chuckle and ready
  mischievous smile

And your safe secure hand folded around
  mine

Gran, you billow graciously over the horizon
  of my life -

A shining fluffy cloud of my childhood

Tinted now with shimmering shades of
  glowing love

An archetype of everything that Grans are
meant to be.

Forty Four

I rise to greet the day on condor wings
Half asleep and half awake
Amidst the fluttering veil
Of Amazonian dreams

I turn to gaze across the landscape past
Part hidden and part revealed
Beneath the carpeted green
Of expeditions trod

I see the cairn where stones of love were
    placed
Some jagged and some smooth
Upon the meandering trail
Of intertwining fates

I hear the echoed tale of lost and found
With strangers and with new friends
Upon the unexpected flight
Of misadventures led

I feel the shadow of missed paths and tasks
Not taken and not fulfilled
Among the refracted maze
Of industrious grind

I touch the shape of memories crafted
On islands and on mountains
Within the squares of power
And sun spirals of art

I turn to gaze at the stretched horizon
Part misty and part defined
Beyond the boundaries mapped
Of predetermined ends

I rise to greet the year on thermal winds
Half afraid and half inspired
Above the flickering flames
Of unquenchable hope.

Orbits

For scarce hours, friendly and warm,
Like the smoulder of a wood-burning stove;
Our lives overlapped in sync -
A strange warp of time and space

Banter reverberating around the kitchen,
Like the rhythmic drone of didgeridoo;
Music lacing brick and tile -
A fountain, a mirror-loch, a trickling spring

Tales of travels and rainbow cultures,
Like meridians across the Earth;
Pricks of experiences remembered -
Needles connecting latitudes of energy

Stars shine brightly in the dark Scottish
    sky,
Like a cosmic dance in step;

Their light winks over the fair Cape
in time -
A promise of orbits to cross again soon

Building Stone Upon Stone

Scotland and Ireland

For many moons have gathered now
People from different lands
Around a table carved from wood
Searching to understand
Why we choke the Earth and Sky
The Rivers and the Seas
And why there is injustice still
And social inequity

We've travelled over land and sea
And around the jewel of Eire
With its walls of stone and sacred sites
And people to inspire
Our pilgrimage across the hills
Is also one within
For we know: before the world can change
With ourselves we must begin

When we go our different ways
We'll take all that we've learned
And try to realise the better world
For which we yearn
And the Celtic knot may join us still
Through the vision that we share
That all life is connected and
Needs our love and care

We have grown, we have grown
Building stone upon stone
A foundation of hope for tomorrow
We have grown, we have grown
And though our future's unknown
Every ending is just another beginning

Footprints

Laughing, smiling, making jokes
Dreams, desires, fleeting hopes
Not defined, not quite clear
Not quite far, not quite near
Out of reach, close at hand
Sets of prints upon the sand
Follow now and now to lead
Now to give and now to need
Perhaps in time, in time I'll know
Where those footprints are to go

Love the Landscape of Your Life

Love the landscape of your life –
It is shaped for you alone
Trust the terrain on which you tread –
Its pathways will lead you home

As you pause for breath
Upon your trail on this Earth
There is much reason to linger and savour:
The vistas and views
The companions you keep
The blessings you hold in your favour

And the cairn tall beside you
Built stone upon stone
Is the beacon to your adventures and
    travels:
'Cross mountain and bushveld
Through desert and forest ...
And within ... as the journey unravels

But tarry not long
For the track lies before you
And the expedition is far from its end:
The mountains they beckon
The trees whisper welcome
In new lands which await 'round the bend

Love the landscape of your life –
It is shaped for you alone
Trust the terrain on which you tread –
Its pathways will lead you home.

Forty Five

The turn of the seasons, the loop of the sun

Another year over, another begun

A decade ago, I felt barely alive

Now, healthy and happy, I turn forty-five

I've searched for new answers to questions
of old

I've dared to be different and dreamed to be
bold

I've tickled life's wonder and kindled love's
spark

I've travelled to places that each left their
mark

The mountain cathedrals of Peja's great
charm

The hills of Sri Lanka with Buddha-blessed
calm

The joining together with Amazon friends

The fresh new beginnings and reconceived
ends

The nocturnal sparkle of Moscow's Red
Square

The spices and colours of New Delhi's flare

The rejuvenation in the fairest of Capes

The call of adventure and shifting of shapes

I've weaved webs of words to teach and
inspire

I've called on our leaders to change or retire

I've spoken with students of making a dent

I've gone to great cities and learned as I
went

The Singapore gardens with green walls of
flowers

The Caspian welcome with Baku's flame
towers

The Da Vinci artworks Milano unveils

The Stockholm ice bar with its blue winter's
tales

The waffles of Antwerp and Amsterdam's
eye

Ann Arbor's giant cookies and trails in the
    sky

The Tesla electric with still Scarlett pace

The Force reawakens from frontiers of
    space

I've listened to whispers of fate on the
    breeze

I've taken a step on the long walk for trees

I've dreamed of a future where waste is no
    more

I've reached for the circle with life as its
    core

The terrors of Paris; its climate accord

The march of brave migrants across
    Europe's ford

The struggles of many show will to survive

I'm counting my blessings; I've turned forty-
    five.

Live 8 Rap

It's not too late
To join Live 8
To change the fate
Of billions of poor
To do more
To settle the score
On the raw
Deal of the past
At last

We won't take the bait
Of the G8
Stalemate
For too long they've lied
Telling us their hands are tied
But they can't hide
From the rising tide
They know the cure
For sure

Let's speak our voice
We have the choice
To cast off the net
Of crippling debt
To increase aid
And make the trade
Fair and square
If we dare
To care

This is our chance
To dance
To a different tune
To turn up the heat
And feel the beat
Of Africa's drum
The silent hum
Of those who refuse
To succumb

This is the time
To rhyme

For a better life

To end the strife

That's rife

To make our mark

And take our part

In walking the path

With a heart

Let this be

Our plea

For the rebirth

Of earth

To make poverty history

To shape a new destiny

This is the space

To take our place

In the human race

This is the tipping point

To heal the disjoint

Of separation

To make reparation

For exploitation

And close the gap

On the map

To open our souls to the tap

Of the Live 8 rap.

Birthday Train

Throw your hands up in the air
Run around without a care
Ask for wishes to come true
In everything you say and do
Enjoy the sunshine and the rain
'Cos nothing stops the birthday train.

Birthday Truck

Jump and dance and roll your eyes

Chase the garden flutterbys

Play with bunches of balloons

Sing aloud your favourite tunes

Wish yourself the best of luck

'Cos nothing stops the birthday truck!

Blurred Vision

It was just a glimpse at first
But enough to look twice
Enough to spark intrigue
To prick my senses
Burst my bubble
An intruder
Alert

She floated in the distance
A figure out of focus
Blurred at the edges
Defying definition
A form in flow
A chimera
Alive

It's not that she was perfect
And I never saw her face
But she fit the moment
Echoed my longing

Spinning in sync
A coincidence
Aware

She passed without knowing
That I wanted to reach out
From fantasy into reality
To touch her knee
Kiss her neck
A butterfly
Alight.

Babies Bounce

Babies bounce
Their laughter is lighter than air
Their dreams as high as the sky
And so they fly
Just as surely as they cry
With worry-free wings
And lives unencumbered

Growing up
Is learning the law of staying down
Giving up on the lullabies of skies
And believing the lies
That the spirit can't rise
On imaginary smoke
And dreams unrequited

Getting wise
Is learning the art of not knowing
Giving up on the clutter of stuff
And saying enough

Of the bluster and bluff

That anchors you down

With things unimportant

Elders float

Their knowing is buoyant as balsa

Their memories like corks on the seas

And so with all ease

They free-ride the breeze

With discarded ballast

And flight rediscovered.

Fractal Faces

I. Beauty

I see the world in your face –
The echoes of your homeland
The whispers of your past
The long song of your people
The memories made to last

I see a face of beauty –
Cheerful and chubby
Tearful and grubby
Tender and twinkly
Crumpled and crinkly

I see you in the morning
I see you late at night
I see you when I'm dreaming
I see you bathed in light

II. Despair

I see the journey in your face –
The first steps of wonder
The twists from the start
The turns of discovery
The path of your heart

I see a face of despair –
Worn out and weary
Beaten and bleary
Rough shod and ragged
Haunted and haggard

I see you in the ghetto
I see you on the street
I see you on the TV
I see you when we meet

III. Hope

I see the story in your face –
The quest for the answers
The courage to fight
The battle of forces
The dark and the light

I see a face of hope –
Wide-eyed and wondrous
Inspired and ponderous
Grateful and giving
Faithful and living

I see you in the city
I see you in the class
I see in the village
I see you when we pass

IV. Freedom

I see nature in your face –
The soil in your skin
The wild in your guise
The rain in your laughter
The sun in your eyes

I see a face of freedom –
Bewildered and bemused
Engaged and enthused
Innovating and learning
Forever sojourning

I see you in the cradle
I see you through the mist
I see you on the wifi
I'm glad that you exist

V. Love

I see the world in your face –
The colours of your palette
The brush marks of your sorrow
The radiance of your vision
The portrait of your tomorrow

I see a face of love –
Compassionate and caring
Shouldering and sharing
Nurturing and feeding
Giving without needing

I see you in the maelstrom
I see you with your smile
I see you in each face I see
You make this life worthwhile.

'Tis the Season

Another cosy Christmas spent
Another year, how quick it went
And now, a short, well-earned respite
Before the clock is rewound tight.

Cherry Hinton Days

One day, I expect, we'll look back and smile
At these blossoming Cherry Hinton days
With walks, traced in chalks, to the
    crumbling cliffs
Of the limestone quarry's white blaze

Some day, may it be, we'll pause for a while
And remember our bright mosaic ways
With strolls, in the knolls of the Gogmagog
    hills
And spoils from the Burylane's maze

One day, I can tell, we'll turn back the dial
To these sun-splintered Cambridge lit days
Getting trim, at the gym, and Saturday
    tennis
And The Orchard, for scones and a laze

One day, mark my words, we'll look back
    and smile
At these swan-sailing Cam river days

Bikes flashing, oars splashing, to the
  syncing of strokes

And the cows on the common at graze.

My Father's Son

We've come a great long way together
Upon the trail of father and son
We've chased the flight of Illusions' feather
And watched the swirling Tao stream run.

From cradling safety in your arms
To infant hugs down on the beach
And catapulting shoulder dives –
Your love was never out of reach.

Then as I grew from boy to man
You placed a compass in my hand –
A set of values and ideals
That point true North in every land.

I watched and learned, as patient deeds
Turned dreams into reality
You taught me that hard work and faith
Grow seeds defying gravity.

So many worlds we've seen together

So many things we've dared and done

I love you always and forever

I'm proud to be my father's son.

The Migrant's Lament

I am the crosser of borders
I am the sailor of seas
I am the cargo of smugglers
I am the hunted who flees

I travelled from cradles of violence
I travelled on paths full of grace
I travelled from terrors of nightmares
I travelled to dreams of this place

I echo your pattern of history
I foretell your future to come
I sleep in the cold of your shadow
I crave for the warmth of your sun

I do not come to make trouble
I do not come here to steal
I bring you the gift of my culture
I need but a moment to heal

I am the wilful survivor
I am the ghost of your fears
I am the triumph of spirit
I am the stain of your tears

I journeyed from harbours of safety
I journeyed on oceans unknown
I journeyed from homesteads of loving
I journeyed to new skies unflown

I wish for the same things you wish for
I share the same sadness and griefs
I strive for the life that you strive for
I don't wish to change your beliefs

I do not come empty handed
I do not come here to take
I bring you the wealth of my talents
I need but a chance to remake

I am the story of ages
I am the angel of new
I am the bringer of changes
I am the migrant – like you.

www.ingramcontent.com/pod-product-compliance
Lightning Source LLC
Chambersburg PA
CBHW072010040426

42447CB00009B/1567